WRITE YOUR FAMILY STORY

Even if you're not a writer
You don't have time
And you don't know where to start

ANITA KULINA

WRITE YOUR FAMILY STORY
Even if you're not a writer
You don't have time
And you don't know where to start

by Anita Kulina

Published by Brandt Street Press

ISBN 978-1-950836-02-4

Library of Congress Control Number: 2025925160

COVER & INTERIOR DESIGN
Mike Murray, pearhouse.com

TABLE OF CONTENTS

THE IMPORTANCE OF EVERYDAYS

Our lives are built on *everydays*, one on top of the other. If I want to know you, really know you, I need your everyday.

Tell me where you worked and give me your job title, and that will give me facts about you. Facts are fine, but they don't tell me enough. What I really want, what I need, is your everyday.

How long did it take you to get ready to go to work in the morning? What did you wear?

Did you take a bus to get to work? Did you drive? Did you walk? Was it a short distance, or a long distance? Did you listen to the radio on the way? Did you talk with a friend?

Who did you say good morning to when you got to work?

Where did you eat lunch? Were you by yourself, or with friends?

Tell me about a time you got angry at work.

Tell me about something that made you sad.

Tell me about a day that was completely exhausting.

Tell me about something that went really, really well. Were you noticed for your achievement?

How did you know it was time to leave that job? Are you proud you worked there, or glad you left? Was it just a job, or more than a job to you?

See what I mean? Your story, the REAL story, is revealed in the everyday.

HOW IT WORKS

STORYTELLING THE EVERYDAY

When you think of your family, what's the first food you think of?

Suppose you write the name of that food at the top of a blank page. And then you write about that food. Just three or four sentences. The first things that come to mind.

Now suppose you find a picture to illustrate what you just wrote about. A picture of the food. A picture of the kitchen or dining room where it's made, or where it's eaten. Or maybe a picture of the person who always makes that food, or the restaurant where it's served.

Grandma's Oatmeal

Grandma had an apple tree in her yard. The apples were tart, but she would sweeten them with brown sugar. She'd put a bowl of apple slices in the center of the table, and we were allowed to put as many apples on our oatmeal as we liked. Sometimes I had more apples than oatmeal!

Fish Sticks

We were Catholic, and it was pre-Vatican II, so we couldn't eat meat on Fridays or during Lent. Instead, we had spaghetti, or fried cabbage, or tuna fish and noodles, or anything else my mother could think of.

My favorite Lenten dinner was Mrs. Paul's Fish Sticks with Kraft Macaroni and Cheese. Giving up meat was intended to be a sacrifice, so it seemed odd to me that I loved fish sticks and macaroni and cheese so much.

You see what's going on here, right? We're not just talking about food.

We're talking about tradition.

We're talking about the everyday moments in our lives that make it rich and happy and sad and exciting and horrible and wonderful and heartbreaking and full of mischief and full of generosity and full of love.

We're talking about the little things that build themselves into the giant things that we carry around for generations ahead.

We're talking about the giant events that become little moments in the center of our hearts.

We're talking about our lives.

We're talking about our history.

This is your family story.

This is where it lives.

In these everyday moments.

COLLECTING YOUR FAMILY STORIES

You can record your family story in ANY WAY YOU CHOOSE.

Take an old-fashioned approach. Paste your photos and stories into a scrapbook.

Create one page at a time on your computer or phone so you can someday send the page to everyone you want to share it with.

Pull your one-page stories together into a small collection, or a larger collection.

Point your phone's camera at a photo and press the video button. Read the story that accompanies the photo. Now you have a video to text your grandson!

Whichever way you choose, that's the right way to do it.

There's no wrong way to write your family story.

To get the younger people in your family interested, think about serving them family history in bite-sized chunks. That's how they're used to getting information. Write your stories to fit their world, and they may surprise you with how receptive they are.

DEFINING FAMILY

How do you define family?

"That's simple. It's my blood relatives. They're my family."

"My family is the people who raised me."

"The people who pick me up when I fall, the ones who are always there for me – always – and I'm always there for them. I don't care if I knew them all my life, or I met them last year. Those people are my family."

"My family began the day I got married, the day I had my children. My life before that was just a prelude."

How you define family is completely up to you. Every definition is valid.

Writing a family history for a blended family, or a chosen family made of people you love, can be an especially rewarding endeavor. You didn't know these people all your life, and there is so much for you to learn! Ask lots of questions, and be prepared to hear some great stories.

SHARING YOUR STORIES

It's so much fun to share family stories. Don't wait until you're done writing. Share each story as you go along!

Send a text to your niece with the story about how her parents met.

Email a PDF to your cousin about the mysterious photo from Jamaica, the one you stumbled on while cleaning out Grandma's wardrobe.

Send your sister's kid that story about the great-uncle they never knew, the one who drove Marilyn Monroe to the USO show when he was in the Navy.

Don't hold on to the stories. Share them!

Create A Sharing Circle

Here are some ideas to get started with sharing your stories.

Set up a group text with your relatives. You'll quickly learn who'd like to chat about family history. Pull those people into a smaller group where you can all share your stories.

Create an email group of friends from your old neighborhood. Chatting with old friends is a wonderful way to bring back memories.

Send a story to a sister or brother or friend. Send the next story to an uncle or a cousin. Send the next story to a grandson.

Find a person, or two, or three who would like to write their own family story. Share your stories with them, and invite them to share their stories with you.

Create a family history writing group. Every time you meet, each person shares a story with the group. Encourage each other by telling the writer what you love about each story.

Share this book with a relative, and create a pipeline between the two of you to collect your family stories and keep them for future generations.

A NOTE ABOUT PDFs

PDF is the archival software used by libraries. It will be around long after Word and Pages and Google Docs are obsolete. That's why I suggest saving your family story in PDFs. There's a specific type of archival PDF that libraries use, and you can search online if you want to learn more about it. The regular PDF is fine for what we're doing here.

So, if you write on a computer or another electronic device, create your family stories in your favorite software and, when you're done, convert the document to a PDF. If you don't know how to create a PDF, a simple internet search will give you the instructions. Or better yet, ask your niece or the neighbor's kid to teach you.

If you're wondering about the best way to collect everything together, I usually recommend creating a 16-page PDF. It's an easily achievable goal. It's long enough to have bound into book form if you like – 16 pages is the minimum amount a digital print shop will probably need to bind it – and yet it's short enough that your grandkids can read it on their phone.

If you're an ambitious writer and planning to write a traditional book, 16-page PDFs are a handy way to explore ideas for that project.

Grandma's Secret Adventure

We found this photo in the back of Grandma's wardrobe. It was in a pale straw purse with the word Jamaica woven onto it in green.

Grandma used to brag that she was a proud Kentuckian and would never leave the farm. We thought that meant she had never left Kentucky.

None of us knows anything about this photo, but we would all like to know!

THE MOST IMPORTANT THING YOU WILL LEARN IN THIS BOOK

There's no wrong way to write your family story.

It doesn't matter if it's perfect.

It only matters that you *do* it.

SPARKING

MEMORIES

HOW TO LOOK AT A PHOTO

Find a picture of yourself from your childhood. Not a portrait. Find a different photo that shows your everyday life: your house, your backyard, your living room, your car, your pet.

When you have the photo in front of you, look at yourself in the photo.

Look at your facial expression. Do you remember this photo being taken? Do you remember what you were feeling?

How are you dressed? Did you always dress like that, or was this for a particular occasion?

Where was this photo taken? Do you remember what it felt like to be in that place?

What did it smell like there? Is there a scent you remember?

What were the sounds in that place?

In a photo, we only see what is seen by the person taking the photo. If we were really there, what would we see beyond that?

You can look at any photo in this way. Even the old photos in your grandfather's drawer, those pictures full of people you never heard of.

Always try to find the photo with a background, if one is available. A front porch, a backyard, an indoor room can tell you a lot.

Even if you've never met the people in the photo, you can draw upon the little tidbits you may have learned about them. You probably know more than you think you do. Use what you see in the photo, as well as the things you already know.

Notice the location. Where are the people in the photo, or where do they seem to be? Could this be a place you recognize, or a place you've heard about?

How are the people dressed? Take a close look at their clothing. Clothing can tell you a lot.

Study their faces closely. Can you read anything from their expressions? What about their posture? In older photos, people often didn't smile. But look at their eyes. You can often read expressions through the eyes.

Does going through these photos make you think of your dad, or your grandma, or someone else in your life who is no longer around? Are you wishing you had asked more questions years ago?

It's not too late. Is their best friend still alive? The people they worked with? Their neighbors? Their schoolfriends? Use your imagination. Who might know more?

WHAT IF I DON'T HAVE PHOTOS?

That's okay, it really is. You have memories, and they're all you really need.

Follow the directions in each of the following approaches, while picturing your grandma's porch or your second-grade classroom or Uncle Teddy's Cadillac. If you like, you can use the *4-Minute Story Cloud* on page 23 or the *Deep Dive* on page 25 to create a clearer snapshot in your mind.

You can also go online to find an image that will illustrate the story you just told. A picture of a Cadillac. A photo of a classroom that looks like the one you remember. The logo from the theater where you had your first date. A photo of a kitten that looks just like little Shadow.

If Grandma's house is still standing, you might be able to find it online. Type her address into a search engine and see what happens.

• • •

Finding images to use online can be
a tricky business. It's perfectly okay
to use some images, and it's not
okay at all to use others. It's all about
copyright. Type "how do I know
which online images I can use" into
your search engine to learn more.

• • •

THE 4-MINUTE STORY CLOUD

A 4-Minute Story Cloud is an easy way to splash your memories onto a page. No one but you is going to read it, so you don't need to worry about grammar or spelling. Or sentence structure. Or even sentences, for that matter.

Take a clean sheet of paper, or create a new document on your computer.

Set a timer on your phone, or your kitchen timer, for four minutes, but don't press Start yet.

At the top of your page, write the topic you chose to write about. Put down your pen and read the next instructions carefully.

You're going to write everything you think of for four minutes. You'll probably write for the full four minutes about the topic you chose, but don't be surprised if you start writing about that topic and the next thing you know, you're writing about your neighbor's dog. That's fine. Honestly. THAT'S PERFECTLY FINE.

The important thing in this exercise is to NEVER STOP WRITING until the timer goes off. If you can't think of anything to write, write the word "and" until a new sentence starts.

I can't emphasize this enough. DON'T STOP WRITING. WRITE FOR THE FULL FOUR MINUTES.

Okay, pick up the pen. Set the timer. Begin. NOW!

Do you usually use your computer to write? Try using a pen and paper. Or vice versa. Research shows it can make a difference in the way you access your memories.

THE DEEP DIVE

Get a clean sheet of paper, or open a new document on your computer.

Set a timer for 12 minutes. Don't hit Start yet. Before you write, we're going to travel back in time.

Think of a place you'd like to travel back to.

Got your place?

Go to <u>anitakulina.com/deep-dive</u>. Put your hands in your lap and mentally answer each of the questions as they are asked. **Don't write anything,** just listen and remember. (If for some reason it's inconvenient to use the internet right now, read the questions that follow and answer them in your mind, one by one.)

Remember, you're not writing yet. You're just traveling back in time.

When you're finished with the memory exercise, start the timer. You're going to write for 12 minutes. Begin your first sentence with "I am…"

I am seven and I'm in Mom's lap while she's reading The Cat in the Hat.

I am sitting next to Grandpa at my first dinner in a fancy restaurant.

I am on the back porch playing with Buster while Papa tends to his tomatoes.

Write until the 12 minutes are up.

If you can't visit the website at the moment, here's a transcript of the Deep Dive. Give yourself time between each question to remember.

- Picture yourself on a particular day, at a particular point in time.

- What are you doing at that very moment on that day?

- What is your posture? Are you standing? Sitting? Are you moving, or are you still?

- What are you wearing?

- What does the air smell like?

- What are the colors you see?

- What are the objects and structures you see around you?

- What are you touching? Think about your whole body. What are your feet touching? Your hands? What are the tactile sensations you feel?

- Look directly in front of you. What do you see? Look a little farther beyond that. What's way out there?

- Turn to your right. What do you see?

- Turn to your left. What do you see?

- Turn all the way around now, so you're looking behind you. What's back there, what's behind you?

- What sounds do you hear? Is there a sound there you haven't heard in a long, long time?

- How do you feel inside? What's going on in your heart?

APPROACHES

There are so many ways to tell a family story, it's hard to know where to start sometimes.

That's why I've written this book. On the following pages, you'll find eleven different approaches. They're all easy and they're all fun.

You can do one of them, or you can do them all. Or anything in between. Many approaches can even be used more than once. (You'll see what I mean when you get started.)

Each approach explores a different facet of your family history. You'll get to see the most important people in your life in new ways, and from different points of view, each time.

Skip around if you like. None of the approaches have to be done in order. Any one you choose will work fine as a place to begin.

Still don't know where to start?
Turn to page 33 and start there.

Research shows when we weave together both negative and positive stories in family history, it fosters emotional resilience and inner strength.

So, don't ever feel like you're obliged to paint a pretty picture. No one else's family is perfect, and nobody is going to believe yours is. Concentrate on the stories you love, but don't be afraid to tell the stories you don't. There's no need to pretend no one in your family ever made an error in judgment or walked down a wrong path.

Think someone can learn from the story? Maybe you ought to write it down.

THE APPROACH:
PEOPLE

This is probably the first approach you think of when you write your family story. And there's a reason for that. It works. It's a simple, effective way of telling the stories of those who came before us, of telling our own stories, and of telling the stories of the up-and-coming generation.

Don't leave out the little ones! Put their story in, even if they're only in second grade. They'll love to see themselves included, and it's a great way to get them interested in family history.

CHOOSE

First, choose who you'd like to write about. Make the selection any way you like.

Choose everyone in your immediate family.

Choose everyone you saw last week at the family reunion.

Choose the people who made their living as farmers, or millworkers, or teachers.

Choose all the people who were homemakers.

Choose everyone who liked to scuba dive.

Choose ten people, or twenty people.

Or five people.

Or one.

It's entirely up to you.

If you can't decide who to choose, start with your immediate family. Then add your grandparents.

SUPPLIES

Find a photo of each person you want to write about, or an image to represent them.

Grab your writing materials – paper and pen, your computer, or even your phone.

That's all you need. Let's get started!

Can't find a photo?

Is there someone else who might have a photo? A family member, a neighbor, a family friend? Is there an image you can use to represent that person, or that time or place?

Still can't find a photo? Go to page 21.

GET IT ONTO THE PAGE

Look at your first photo. Answer these questions. (If you don't know an answer, it's fine to skip that question.)

Who is this?
When were they born?
Where did they grow up?
Where did they go to school?
What were they really good at?
What did they do for fun?
What did you learn from them?

If you want to include additional information, go ahead and do so. Your goal is to write four sentences. You can write more if you like, but try to write at least four.

Pair your photo with your sentences.

Repeat this process for each person you chose to write about.

Share your stories with your circle.

NEED TO SPARK A MEMORY?

Go to the *Sparking Memories* section on page 17.

Do a 4-Minute Story Cloud. As your topic, write the person's name at the top of your page.

Do a Deep Dive. As your place, choose the setting of a particular moment you spent with that person.

Uncle Steve was Daddy's older brother. They grew up in a coal town near Pittsburgh, Pennsylvania, that they always referred to as "The Patch." Steve worked in the coal mine as a teen, but after a cave-in he joined the Merchant Marines, where he trained as a chef. When we were children, he sent us gifts during his travels around the world. He was a wonderful cook and taught me how to make Hungarian goulash.

Uncle Jack was on the wrong side of the law. I guess that's a nice way to say that. He was in jail sometimes when we were young, but he was great fun when he was around. Mom was always sweet to him when he came to visit, and she never gave him a hard time about not having a regular job or anything. She told me once he had been in the war, and that was why he was "different," as she put it.

Whenever he came to visit, Uncle Jack had pockets full of Clark Bars for us kids. He always took time to play ball with us before he talked to the grownups. If he sat on the porch to drink beer with Dad, after a while he would start to talk really loud. His daughters seemed a little scared of him, but I never was.

THE APPROACH: COMMON THREADS

Every family has numerous common threads running through it.

That's because…

* * *

Every family has its own unique way
of expressing itself.

* * *

Your family may express itself through a hobby, or a sport. You all may have a lifelong interest in one thing or another. There might be an activity you've been doing for generations, or something you've all picked up recently and dove headlong into.

Whatever it is, your family gravitates toward that thing because it's important to you all.

And it brings you together.

That's what a common thread does.

You have many common threads in your family. If you don't believe me, turn the page and you'll see how easy it is to identify yours.

CHOOSE

Name something that's important to your family.

Maybe your family is really into gardening. Your grandparents, all your aunts and uncles have a garden. Kids grow up working in the garden. Family members exchange seeds. Someone has a greenhouse. There are family trips to the local nursery every spring.

Maybe education is a big thing in your family. Everyone knew they were going to college by the time they were in kindergarten. Conversation at the dinner table was about classes, and prospects for the future. Graduations were important family events.

Maybe your family is really into sports. Or cooking. Or vacations together.

Maybe all these things are important to your family. Maybe plenty more we haven't even mentioned. Pick one for your common thread.

It doesn't matter which one. If you don't know what to choose, just pick the first thing that comes to mind.

Write down the one you chose. Then write a sentence describing how you know it's important to your family.

What did you choose?

That's your common thread.

Are you wondering now, did I pick the right one? Maybe I should have picked another one.

Don't panic. You can change your common thread right now.

You can keep this common thread, and write about another one later.

You can choose a whole new common thread from the next page.

COMMON THREAD IDEAS

*Choose one of these, or use them
to spark an idea of your own.*

A chronological list of places we lived

Family vacations to distant lands

The family cottage at the lake

Our favorite beaches

Schools we each attended, and what we studied there

Family members and their best friends

Our favorite neighbors

Our pets over the years

The pets we all have now

Items associated with each family member: an article of clothing, or something they carried

We love a party

We love to eat

Everyone has a garden

Family game nights

Family movie nights

We love to dance

We love concerts

We love theme parks

We've seen every Marvel movie

These are the churches we attend

These are the clubs we belong to

We love the Pittsburgh Steelers

We love to hike

We love to make art

We love to make music

We're great at crafts

We're all athletic

We never met an animal we didn't like

SUPPLIES

Find some photos or images to match your common thread. There are probably at least a few in your family photo album. Maybe you're all at a baseball game. Maybe you're climbing a mountain in Nepal. Maybe you're sitting on the front porch shelling peas.

Gather as many photos as you like. Aim for at least six.

Grab your writing materials – anything from paper and pen, to your computer, or even your phone.

That's all you need. Let's get started!

~~~~~~

Can't find a photo?

Is there someone else who might have a photo? A family member, a neighbor, a family friend? Is there an image on the internet you can use to represent your common thread?

~~~~~~

GET IT ONTO THE PAGE

Look at your first photo. Examine it carefully, gathering all the information you can from it. (For tips on examining a photo, go to page 19.)

Try to remember everything you can about the photo and the memories surrounding it. If you need help, go to the *Need to Spark a Memory?* suggestions that follow.

Your goal is to write four sentences. You can write more if you like, but try to write at least four.

Pair your photo with what you just wrote.

Repeat this process for each photo.

Share your stories with your circle.

NEED TO SPARK A MEMORY?

Go to the *Sparking Memories* section on page 17.

Do a 4-Minute Story Cloud. For your topic, choose an item or place related to your common thread.

Do a Deep Dive. For your topic, choose a place or an event related to your common thread.

Grandma's Purse

Grandma carried a purse. It was a big purse, but not too big. She told us how you could tell. When you held it with your arm extended downward, if the purse touched the ground, it was too big for you. Grandma's purse was always the right size. The purse had to match her shoes, too. This was a must.

Inside the purse was a handkerchief, a rosary, her house key and a little black change purse, dollar bills folded firmly inside. On Sundays, Grandma's purse also held her prayer book, so she could read the prayers for Mass in her native Polish.

This picture was taken after our neighbors – Johnny and Margie – returned from Ocean City after vacationing with some of their nieces and nephews who were a bit older than us. We were excited, of course, to get new T-shirts because we didn't have much when we were growing up and usually wore a lot of hand-me-downs. I loved mine because it proclaimed that I was a Little Angel. (Sandie didn't fare as well – that Little Devil!)

Looking at this picture now emphasizes how much Johnny, Margie and their family meant to us. They weren't just people you talked with occasionally in passing. They had us over every Christmas season and had gifts for us kids, took us up to Conneaut Lake to ride in Johnny's boat, babysat whenever needed and were always there for all of us. We knew their whole extended family and they knew ours. I hope they knew how much they meant to all of us.

THE APPROACH:
TRADITIONS

Traditions can last a few years, or they can last for generations. Sometimes we forget that those old-time traditions we look back on so fondly were once brand new. Everything starts somewhere.

Certain traditions are simple. My husband calls his mom every Sunday at 6 p.m. Maybe your family orders pizza and watches a movie on Friday nights. If you do something on a regular basis, it becomes a tradition. Like shopping for school clothes every fall. Or eating cherry popsicles on the back deck on the Fourth of July.

When you were a kid, did your dad take you to McDonald's on Saturdays for a Happy Meal? Did your aunts come to all your soccer games and root for you from the stands? When you smile about those afternoons, you're remembering your traditions.

Traditions are like anchors in a family. Traditions make us feel that we are part of a whole.

In my family, when it's your birthday, everyone calls you and sings "Happy Birthday" to you over the phone. This has spread into my husband's family as well now. It's one of our traditions. Those calls say *Happy birthday,* but they also say, *You're part of this family. We are better together.*

That's what a tradition does. That's the anchor part of it.

• • •

Traditions are like anchors in a family.
Traditions make us feel that we are
part of a whole.

• • •

CHOOSE

Make a list of your family traditions. They can include traditions that have been in your family for generations, or they can be traditions that began last year, or last month. They can be traditions you had in the past for a short but important period of time, or they can still be happening now.

Challenge yourself to come up with at least six, though you may find you have many more!

~~~~~~

It's not cheating to ask family members
if they can add to your list.

~~~~~~

SUPPLIES

Find a picture to reflect each tradition. There are probably at least a few in your family photo album or in your social media accounts. Maybe you're all at the theater on opening night of the new Star Wars movie. Maybe all the uncles are playing horseshoes at the Memorial Day barbecue. Maybe everyone is in their pajamas on Saturday morning watching cartoons. If you don't have a photo, find an image to represent that tradition.

Grab your writing materials – anything from paper and pen, to your computer, or even your phone.

That's all you need. Let's get started!

Can't find a photo?

Is there someone else who might have a photo? A family member, a neighbor, a family friend?

Still can't find a photo? Go to page 21.

GET IT ONTO THE PAGE

Look at your first photo. Examine it carefully. Try to remember everything you can about the photo and the memories surrounding it. If you need help, see the *Need to Spark a Memory?* section that follows.

Your goal is to write four sentences. You can write more if you like, but try to write at least four.

Pair your photo with what you just wrote.

Repeat this process for each photo you chose.

Share your stories with your circle.

NEED TO SPARK A MEMORY?

Go to the *Sparking Memories* section on page 17.

Do a 4-Minute Story Cloud. Choose a tradition that involves two people (or three or four) as your topic.

Do a Deep Dive. Choose a big event, or a tradition that involves many people, as your topic.

Sunday Mornings

Everyone went to church in our family, like it or not. Mummy always said our souls were her responsibility until we turned 18, at which point it would be us and not her who went to hell for our sins. So off we trotted every Sunday morning.

Mum went to 9 o'clock Mass with the little kids. We teens and preteens went to the 10:30, the one that had the handsome priest who gave short sermons and never made you feel bad. Daddy ushered at 12:15 Mass.

In late fall or early winter, right around Thanksgiving, CBS would have a special national broadcast of "The Wizard of Oz." This was a big deal in households with children, and ours was no exception. We would get excited as soon as we learned which day it would be shown. Mom would buy Rice Krispies and marshmallows to make us Marshmallow Treats, which we only had once a year for this special occasion.

On Wizard of Oz day, we gathered around the television in the living room, Mom with us in her rocking chair because she was a big Judy Garland fan and loved when she sang "Over the Rainbow." We kids were all scared of the witch and especially the flying monkeys, but we all loved the movie and wouldn't miss it for anything.

THE APPROACH: FAMILY VALUES

One of the things that holds your family together is its shared values. These are the things you all agree on, even when you don't agree on anything else. The things you know to be true, deep in your heart. The things that are important. The things every member of your family brings to the world around them.

As you read this, you're probably already exploring what your family's values might be. So, turn the page and get started!

* * *

Shared values are the things you all agree on, even when you don't agree on anything else.

* * *

CHOOSE

Make a list of members of your family. Include extended family members, if you like. Make the list as long or as short as you want.

Be sure to put your own name on the list, too!

SUPPLIES

Find a photo of your family, or an image to represent your family.

Grab your writing materials – paper and pen, your computer, or even your phone.

That's all you need. Let's get started!

GET IT ONTO THE PAGE

Ask yourself, what are the three things my family values most? Write those values after your name.

Now contact the first person on your list and ask them, *What are the three things our family values most?* Be sure NOT to tell them what you chose before you ask them what they would choose.

When you have their answer, write those values next to their name on your list.

Call the next person, and the next person, and the next. Ask them the same question.

When you've contacted everyone, look over all the answers.

Now make a second list of the values that show up most often. Feel free to include a value that only shows up once but is close to your heart!

When you have the list of values, make a poster.

Share the poster with your family.

Jackson
Family Values

FAITH
EDUCATION
TIDINESS
HUMILITY
INNER STRENGTH

Czinke
Family Values

Kindness
Generosity
Hard Work

Family is everything!

THE APPROACH:
HOW THEY MET

Every family has stories you haven't heard, stories that are hidden in plain sight. All you need to do is ask.

With this approach, we ask family members a simple question about someone who's important in their lives. Whether it's a friend or family member, a romantic partner or a new addition, there's a story behind the first moments they shared together. A story that will reveal a little more about your family, who you are collectively, and who's important in your world.

Always feel free to include family friends in your stories. Who we are friends with says a lot about who we are.

CHOOSE

Choose two people you can get in touch with. They must be in a relationship, but it can be any kind of a relationship. Some examples:

- *Your husband and his best friend*
- *Your son and daughter-in-law*
- *Your mom and dad*
- *Your sister and her wife*
- *The children in your blended family*
- *Your brother and his girlfriend*
- *Your granddaughter and her best friend*

This would also be a lovely time to recall the meeting of a parent and child. Ask your brother about the day his daughter was born. To get a fuller picture, ask her mother, too!

SUPPLIES

Find a photo of the people you chose. If you don't have a photo, find an image to represent their relationship. Or take a photo when you see them!

Grab your phone or another recording device, and your writing materials: paper and pen, your computer, or whatever you use to write.

You may want to consider recording your conversations. I'm so glad I recorded the stories my mother told me. When someone is gone, it's such a lovely thing to hear their voice again!

I mention this not to make you wish you'd recorded people who are gone, but to make you think of future generations. Your sister's great-grandkids might love to hear her voice many years from now. And someone might love to hear yours!

Remember to tell someone you'd like to record them before you begin. It's not only common courtesy, but in some states it's actually illegal to record someone without their permission.

GET IT ONTO THE PAGE

Your aim is to get the How They Met story from both points of view.

That means contacting the first person you chose and asking, *How did you two meet?* Record your conversation, or take notes. Ask questions when it seems appropriate. *Which bus were you riding when he sat next to you? Do you remember what you were wearing? Do you remember the first thing you said to each other?*

When you've spoken to the first person, contact the second person. DO NOT mention anything the first person said. Simply ask the same question: *How did you two meet?*

WHEN YOU HAVE BOTH STORIES

If the stories are similar, combine them to make one complete story. You can use their exact words, or tell the story in your own words. Whichever is easiest is fine.

If the stories differ, tell each story separately. Use their own words as much as you like.

You only need a few sentences. Three or four should do it.

Pair your story with the photo you selected.

Share the story with your circle.

NEED TO SPARK A MEMORY?

If you'd like to write a How They Met story about your own relationships, go to the *Sparking Memories* section on page 17.

Do a 4-Minute Story Cloud about your best friend in high school.

Do a Deep Dive about the day you met someone who became very important in your life.

How They Met

Aunt Sherri

I knew Bobby from when we were little. I used to hang out with his sister Vanessa. He never paid any attention to me, but I always thought he was cute because he read books all the time and I liked those intelligent boys. I don't think he ever talked to me, though, until we were in our twenties and I ran into him at Marshall's Tavern on Streets Run Road. He was with a group of friends from school and he asked me to dance. He was a good dancer. I had never seen him dance before.

Uncle Bobby

The first time I remember talking to your Aunt Sherri, we were probably 12 or 13. I was reading *The Lord of the Flies* for school, and she had already read it, and she was a year behind me. She read it just for fun, and I remember being impressed with that.

I found this photo after Nana died. It's the only picture I've ever seen of my grandfather. I know his first name was John because it says so on the back of the photo. I don't know how they met, or anything else about him. When I showed Dad the photo, he told me it was his father, but he wouldn't say anything more. When I asked Mom, she said she doesn't know anything about him. I have a million questions no one wants to answer.

When I look closely at my grandfather's face, I can see my brother Ronnie's smile.

THE APPROACH:
THE BIG EVENT

Surprisingly, an often-overlooked aspect of family storytelling is the important times we gather together. Weddings, family reunions, bar and bat mitzvahs, even funerals are chock-full of stories.

We remember these events, and they become pivotal in our lives, but we often don't think to record our memories. Sure, we might have photographs. Lots of them, usually. Match those photos with recollections and you have something to keep and treasure, something to pass on to future generations.

CHOOSE

Choose an event to write about. It might be your sister's wedding thirty years ago. It might be the trip you took to Las Vegas with your girlfriends. It might be last year's family reunion, or Great-Aunt Beatrice's 100th birthday party, or the fishing trip you took with your dad when you were kids. Any event will work.

Okay, do you have your event?

Your next step is to make a short list of people who attended the event. These should be people you can get in touch with. Try for at least four, but you can add more if you like.

● ● ●

If youngsters attended, it might be fun
to add them to your list!

● ● ●

SUPPLIES

Find a photo, or several photos, of the event. If you don't have photos of the event, locate photos of the people who attended. Or find an image to represent the person or event.

Grab your phone or another recording device, and your writing materials: paper and pen, your computer, or whatever you use to write.

Can't find a photo?

Is there someone else who might have a photo? A family member, a friend? Is there an image you can use to represent the event?

Still can't find a photo? Go to page 21.

GET IT ONTO THE PAGE

Contact everyone on your list separately.

When you speak to each person, ask them what they remember about the event. Don't tell them what you remember, or what anyone else remembered, until they've answered your question.

Record each conversation, or take notes.

Pull four sentences out of the stories each person told you. (You can use more if you like, but try to find at least four.) Use those sentences to tell the story. Match each story with a photo of the event.

Don't forget, you'll want four sentences of your own story, too!

When you're done, share your stories with your circle.

⬤ ⬤ ⬤

This can work especially well with large family events because everyone doesn't get to see everything. You may find you missed a lot of interesting things that happened that day!

⬤ ⬤ ⬤

NEED TO SPARK A MEMORY?

Go to the *Sparking Memories* section on page 17.

Do a 4-Minute Story Cloud. At the top of your page, write the name of someone who attended the event with you.

Do a Deep Dive. Write the name of the event at the top of your page.

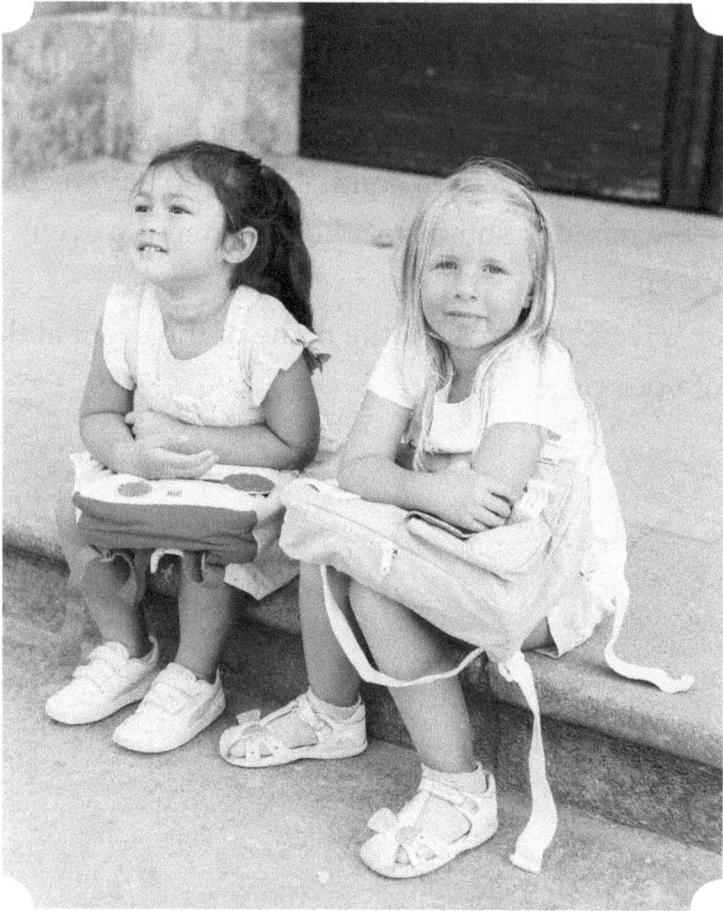

Angela

I don't remember a whole lot about the wedding. I was pretty young. I mostly remember being excited Jessie was my sister now. I know there was a band that played music, and everybody danced. Oh, and there was chocolate cake with red roses on top. And the dress you made me wear was scratchy, but I liked the headband with the flowers on it. I made you let me wear it to school, remember?

Mom wasn't happy about her choral group being booked at the Legion Hall, since she expected they'd be singing for men who were less interested in music and more interested in beer. She was pleasantly surprised to discover we had secretly rented the hall and booked the choral group to sing at her 75th birthday party.

Mom spent the day surrounded by friends from the senior center and neighbors from when we were growing up. The highlight of the day, for many of us, was the singing. Mom's solo was one of her favorites, "Let Me Call You Sweetheart."

THE APPROACH:
THE SPECIAL MOMENT

Some of the most wonderful times in our lives are the ones we don't realize will be wonderful. They're those little moments when a trip to the movies or a dinner out becomes a memory that lives deep within our hearts until the end of time.

In this approach, we'll write about those moments. Those tender moments, those funny moments, those moments that show you that life is special, and surprising, and abundantly full of everything that matters.

CHOOSE

Choose your special moment. You can choose a moment you shared with someone you're still in touch with, or you can choose a moment that you shared with someone no longer around, a moment you hold deeply in your heart.

It can be something simple, like the afternoon you and your sister spent with Grandma making oatmeal cookies.

It can be something big, like the day your husband proposed.

It can be the time you took your daughter to the Taylor Swift concert, and it turned out to be a night neither of you will ever forget.

Whatever you choose is fine. If you can't think of a moment, choose a favorite memory from high school.

SUPPLIES

Find a photo to represent that day. If you don't have a photo of the event itself, locate photos of the people who attended. Or find an image to represent the person or event.

Grab your phone or another recording device, and your writing materials: paper and pen, your computer, or whatever you use to write.

That's all you need. Let's get started!

GET IT ONTO THE PAGE

If you're still in contact with the other person or people from your special moment, contact them and ask what they remember about that day. Don't tell them what you remember until they've told you what they remember.

Record your conversation, or take notes.

Write four sentences to tell the story of the event. You can write more if you like, but try to write at least four.

Match your photo or image with what you wrote.

Share your story with your circle.

NEED TO SPARK A MEMORY?

Go to the *Sparking Memories* section on page 17.

Do a 4-Minute Story Cloud. At the top of your page, write the name of someone involved in your special moment.

Do a Deep Dive. Give a name to your special moment and write it at the top of your page.

Grandma was no-nonsense when it came to baking. Susie and I stayed at Grandma's house all weekend one winter, and we made cookies and challah for family, for her neighbors, and for friends. I remember feeling grown up because I was helping. Grandma gave me an apron and I had to tie it around my waist twice, it was so big.

The house smelled wonderful every day. On Saturday we helped Grandma make chicken soup for dinner, and on Sunday Grandpa went to the deli to get us lunch because Grandma was too tired to cook!

Growing up, none of us had any money, so we only ever went to the amusement park once a year, when we could buy subsidized tickets for the school picnic. Until Dave's dad (who was a bookie) was repaid a debt with a shopping bag full of Kennywood tickets, and suddenly we felt like the richest kids in town.

Over and over again, Dave filled his pockets and invited us to join him. We lived at Kennywood that summer! One afternoon when the park wasn't crowded, Dave and I rode The Racer 27 times.

THE APPROACH: SHOWING LOVE

We all have our own way of showing love to our family.

Sometimes it's really obvious, like how Aunt Sofia brings all the children a new toy when she comes to visit. Or how Uncle Toby always brings you that cake on your birthday, the devil's food with chocolate icing, because he knows it's your absolute favorite.

Sometimes it's not as obvious and you have to look for it. Like how Grandpa attends every one of the kids' soccer games and dance recitals. Or how Aunt Min carefully listens to all the children and gives them her undivided attention.

We all have our own ways of showing love. This approach is an opportunity to celebrate that.

CHOOSE

Make a list of everyone in your immediate family.

Or everyone in your extended family.

Or the people who aren't related who feel like family.

Or the people in your life who make you smile!

It's entirely up to you who you'd like to include.

Add your own name to the list, too!

〰〰〰〰〰〰〰〰〰〰〰〰〰〰

Be sure to include the youngsters on your list!

〰〰〰〰〰〰〰〰〰〰〰〰〰〰

SUPPLIES

Find photos of the people on your list. Or find an image to represent them.

Grab your writing materials – paper and pen, or your computer, or even your phone.

That's all you need. Let's get started!

Can't find a photo?

Is there someone else who might have a photo? A family member, a friend? Is there an image that makes you think of them?

Still can't find a photo? Go to page 21.

GET IT ONTO THE PAGE

After each name on your list, write the way that person shows love to your family.

Maybe you cook food.

Maybe your brother fixes everyone's car.

Maybe your aunt is a big hugger.

Maybe your sister calls people every week just to say hello.

Write two or three sentences about each person's generosity and kindness.

Match your photos with what you wrote about the person.

Share your stories with your circle.

If you're not sure what to write about someone on your list, call a family member and ask how that person has shown them love.

NEED TO SPARK A MEMORY?

Go to the *Sparking Memories* section on page 17.

Do a 4-Minute Story Cloud. At the top of your page, write the name of one of the people on your list.

Do a Deep Dive. As your topic, choose a moment when you showed love to someone in your family.

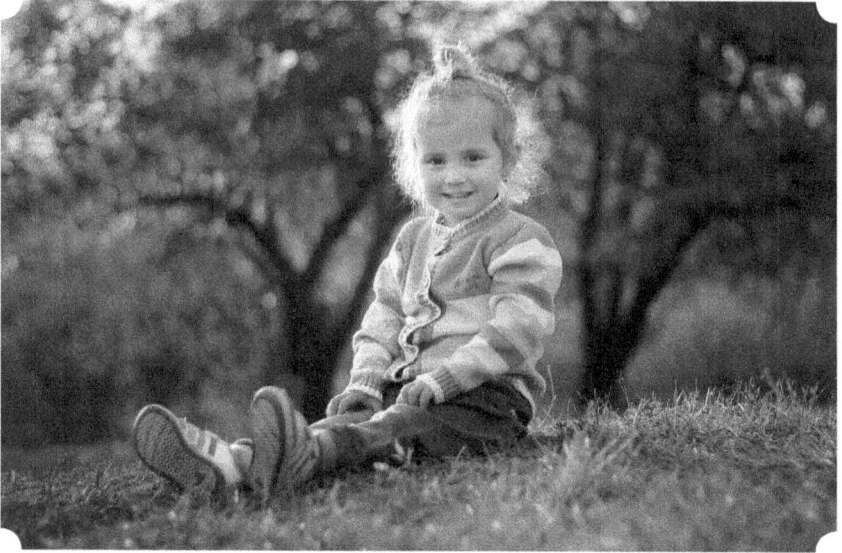

Jeannie is always so generous. Sharing is her middle name. If she's eating a cookie and you walk into the room, she will give you half.

Noah stops in after school sometimes just to say hello. He always has a story to tell that will make us laugh.

THE APPROACH: FAMILY RECIPES

For many of us, family memories revolve around food. Whether it's a cookout or a football game, we already know what food we'll find there. Grandma will make her famous strudel. Stan will have a crockpot full of kielbasa and sauerkraut. Aunt Marina will bring homemade tortilla chips, and Aunt Gina will make the salsa to go with it.

These foods are special to us, not only because we like eating them, but because they make us think of family. When we see these foods, we feel loved. It's as simple as that.

With this approach, we'll use the element of food to tell our family story.

● ● ●

When we see these foods, we feel loved. It's as simple as that.

● ● ●

CHOOSE

List six foods that come to mind when you think of your family. If it's not a breeze to think of six, here are some suggestions.

They don't have to be anything fancy. I loved when my mom made hot dogs and baked beans with fried potatoes when I was a kid. That would go on my list. Maybe your mom served applesauce with every meal, or canned peas, or a glass of milk because "it makes your bones strong." Every one of the foods you choose will have a story to tell.

Maybe your family went out to eat a lot, and there was a favorite restaurant and a favorite dish there. That can go on your list. If you always get birthday cakes from a favorite bakery, that can go on your list.

When my husband was growing up, frozen dinners were a new-fangled thing. Most Sunday nights, his family ate Swanson dinners on TV trays in the living room while they watched *Wild Kingdom*. The kids loved Sunday night dinner. Swanson TV dinners would definitely be on his list.

Still having trouble making your list? Call your family and ask, "What foods do you associate with our family?"

SUPPLIES

Photos of the foods you chose, or a photo of the person who made the food, or the place where you ate it. Or an image to represent any of those things.

Recipes for the foods, if you have them.

Something to write with. Phone, pencil, or whatever you choose.

That's all you need. Let's get started!

GET IT ONTO THE PAGE

Answer these questions about the first food you chose. If you don't know the answer, it's fine to skip to the next question.

Who usually makes this food?

Where did they get the recipe?

When was the first time they made it, or the first time you tasted it?

How often is it made? Is it made for a certain occasion?

How is this food served?

If you have a recipe, read it over carefully to make sure it will be easy for someone else to follow. If your family always uses certain brands in the ingredients, be sure to include that information.

Add your photo or image to what you've written.

Share your story with your circle.

It might be fun to include a memory about this food, the person who made it, or when it was served. If a memory doesn't come to mind, try the *Sparking Memories* section on page 17.

Klops was a frequent supper in the Kulina household on Haldane Street, because it's not only traditional but economical. Klops is a Polish dish, and Mum's recipe came from her family. There are many variations to this recipe. Nancy uses fresh bread rather than saltines, like her mother did years ago. Anita uses seasoned bread crumbs and adds onions to the gravy. This recipe is Cyl's version, and it's the one Melissa and Brian ate while they were growing up.

Klops
2 lbs. hamburger
2 eggs, beaten
1 onion, chopped
1 sleeve of saltines, crumbled
1/4 cup milk
2 envelopes Giant Eagle beef gravy mix
4 or 5 mushrooms, chopped

Stir first five ingredients together in a large bowl until thoroughly combined. If mixture seems dry, add a little more milk. Form into hamburger patties and fry in a covered frying pan with a little water in the bottom. When almost done, add mushrooms. Add beef gravy mix as directed on back of packet. Cook until gravy is thickened. Serve with mashed potatoes.

This recipe can easily be halved or doubled. Klops can be made ahead of time and frozen, and later defrosted and cooked in water and then gravy. It's a good meal for a busy day.

MEMORIES OF POTATO PANCAKES

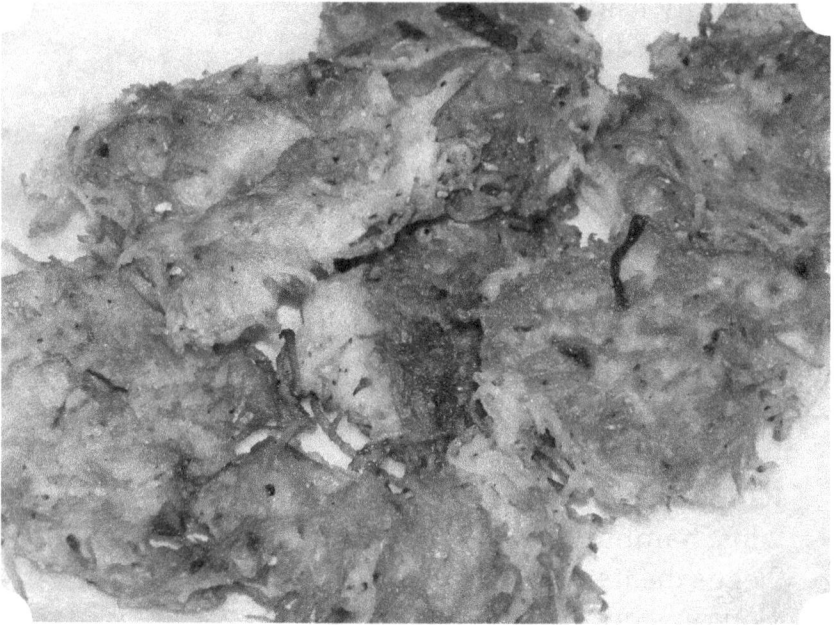

Birthdays always remind me of food. When we were young, my mom always let us choose what she would make for the family dinner. Potato pancakes was always my youngest brother Timmy's choice. It was a lot of work for my mom to make potato pancakes for all eight of us. We didn't have potato pancakes as a side dish, like most people do. It was our main dish, so she made lots, and I mean lots. Mom would peel and use a hand grater to grate about 10 pounds of potatoes and fry them in her cast iron skillets that were blackened from all the many dinners fried in them. If I close my eyes, I can still smell the aroma of the oil and potatoes in the pan. My mom made the very best potato pancakes. Us kids would stand in line to get them before they ever made it to the plate she had with the paper towel to sop up the grease. We would pick the ones we wanted. Some of us liked them a little thicker, others extra crispy. Extra crispy was my favorite.

When we were really young, we had a toy "Mr. Potato Head." Mr. Potato Head was really just a bunch of plastic pieces to make a Mr. Potato Head by adding a hat, ears, mustache, hands and feet, etc. to a potato. When mom would finish grating the potatoes she had, she would holler into the living room for us to return the potatoes we were playing with so she could finish dinner. The Mr. Potato Head toy was later revised to include a plastic potato (I suppose for sanitary purposes), but I don't remember that being as much fun as using a real potato.

We all have mom's recipe for potato pancakes, but I don't know about anyone else in our family, they just don't taste as good as mom's.

THE APPROACH:
YOUR HOME AS FAMILY HISTORY

Like the friends we spend time with, and the clothes we wear, our home tells a lot about us.

I'm not talking about superficial things, like the latest appliances or the most elegant living room. I'm talking about everyday life.

Picture your childhood home, right now, just for a minute. Are there books in the hallway, gardening tools by the back door? Is the living room immaculate and ready for company, or is there a playpen in the corner and a slew of Matchbox cars strewn over the coffee table? What foods are in the refrigerator? What kind of plates are in the cupboard? Do you hear music, or people talking, or any other sounds? When you got home from school, what room did you head to first? Where was your favorite place to sit on a sunny afternoon?

Tell us about your home, and you tell us about your family. It's as simple as that.

Tell us about your home, and
you tell us about your family.

CHOOSE

imagine yourself in your home. You can choose any place you've ever lived, from your home as a child to where you live now.

Got your place?

Now, choose a room. It can be the living room, bedroom, kitchen, any room you want. You can even choose the backyard if you like.

SUPPLIES

A photo of that room, or an image to represent that room. If people are in the photo, that's even better.

Whatever you write with – pen and paper, your computer, or even your phone.

GET IT ONTO THE PAGE

Before you write, take yourself back in time.

Imagine yourself in the room you chose.

Pick a place to stand in the room.

Now turn around very slowly, paying attention to everything you see:

The walls, ceiling, the floor.

The furniture.

All the things on shelves or strewn about.

Any people going in and out.

Pay attention to the colors and textures that surround you.

Are there things in that room you haven't seen for a long time?

Are there things in that room you don't see in a home today?

Write four sentences about the room you chose. You can write more than four, but try for at least four.

Match your photo or image with what you wrote.

Share your story with your circle.

If you like, choose a different room, or a different home, and start again!

NEED TO SPARK A MEMORY?

Go to the *Sparking Memories* section on page 17.

Do a 4-Minute Story Cloud. At the top of your page, write the name of an object in the room you chose.

Do a Deep Dive. Write the name of the room you chose at the top of your page.

Our kitchen was in the back of the house and opened onto the patio, which was really just a cement slab that ran the width of the house. The stove was on one side of the back door and the refrigerator on the other side. The sink was under a window, which Mum always prized because she could look outside as she worked.

The table took up most of the kitchen. It was large enough to hold all eight of us, plus a couple friends or neighbors. It ran along the wall right beyond the door to Mum and Dad's bedroom. If you sat in a chair on that side of the table, you might be blocked in and not be able to get out of your seat to get seconds from the pot on the kitchen stove. Above the table was a picture of The Last Supper. Mummy always sat at one end of the table, Daddy at the other, with all us kids between them.

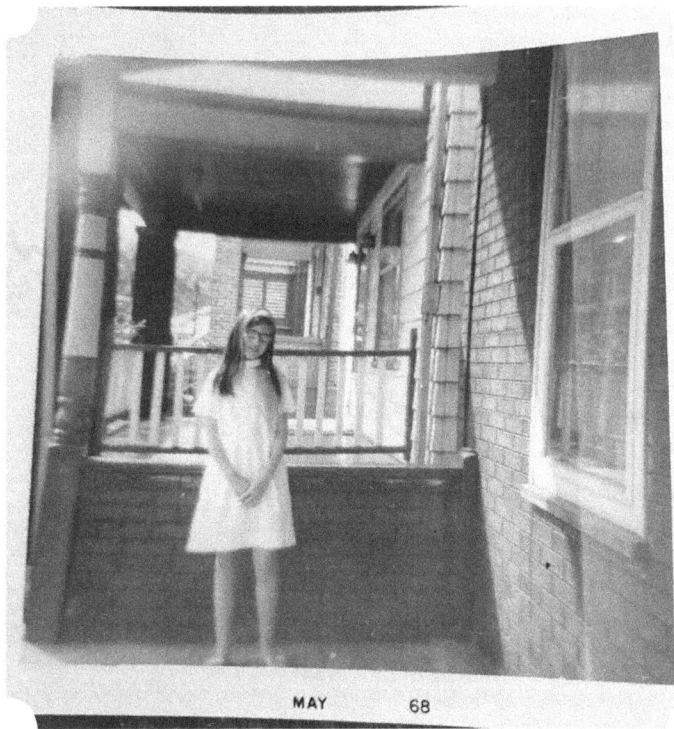

MAY   68

This picture is rare for two reasons. One, we didn't have much money for photographs so they were only taken on special occasions. (This is Nancy at Easter.) Two, because there's only one person on our front porch.

Our house was a gathering place for young people in our neighborhood. At any time of day, you might find a group of little ones waiting for their turn to play hopscotch on our sidewalk. Or a group of middle schoolers reading books on our glider. Or a group of teens playing cards or playing guitar. Or all of them at once!

THE APPROACH:
YOUR LIFE IS FAMILY HISTORY

How do you define history? Here's how I define it. Everything since the day I was born is part of my life. Everything before the day I was born is history.

I bet you feel the same.

That means, to the kids in your life, everything that happened before the day they were born is history. That's most of your life. To your great-great-grandchildren, your entire life is history.

You may think, oh, my story isn't important enough to go in a family history. But think about this.

You'll tell us the story of a time and place, and your reactions to that time and place. Those are the exact things that make history interesting.

We're all interested in other people, what they do, what they think, how they navigate their way through life. Everyday life is especially interesting to anyone whose life is different from yours.

You don't have to write a big, formal memoir or autobiography to record your life. In fact, your family may be more likely to read it in bite-sized chunks!

CHOOSE

Choose six topics from the list below. Or choose three.
Or seven. Or all of them. Or create your own.

- ▣ A play you attended when you were young
- ▣ A television show you watched all the time when you were young
- ▣ A movie you attended when you were young
- ▣ A concert you attended when you were young
- ▣ Any chore you had growing up that kids might not do anymore
  - ✳ Hanging clothes on a clothesline
  - ✳ Helping to can vegetables from the garden
  - ✳ Taking the toaster to the fix-it shop
  - ✳ Taking shoes to the shoemaker to be resoled
- ▣ Your favorite toys as a child
- ▣ Any pastime you don't see kids doing anymore
  - ✳ Roller skating
  - ✳ Playing jacks
  - ✳ Jumping rope
  - ✳ Playing Oregon Trail on a Commodore computer

- Something teens don't do anymore
  - Clap erasers after school
  - Dance to 45s on a portable record player
  - Take a stenography class
  - Wait at home for a phone call
- Any place you worked: a description of the place, who you worked with, what your job entailed
- A historical event during your lifetime
  - Watching the September 11 attacks on television
  - Getting in line to get the new polio vaccine
  - The day your brother came home from the war
  - What it was like to be in lockdown during a pandemic
- Your childhood neighborhood
- The street where you grew up

SUPPLIES

A photo or an image to represent each topic, or a photo of yourself or another person involved in that topic.

Whatever you write with – pen and paper, your computer, or even your phone.

That's all you need. Let's get started!

GET IT ONTO THE PAGE

Write four sentences about the first topic you chose. You can write more than four, but try for at least four. If you need a memory boost, try the *Sparking Memories* section on page 17.

Match your photo or image with what you wrote.

Repeat with each topic.

Share your stories with your circle.

The first concert I ever went to was when Pete Seeger came to Pittsburgh. I think he played at Carnegie Music Hall. He was touring the country to support the grape boycott by the migrant workers, led by Cesar Chavez.

I was probably fourteen. I had never been to a concert before and didn't know what to expect. Pete came on stage and taught us a song. The whole audience joined in. Then he taught us another, and another. We sang through most of the concert. It was a blast.

When I got home that night, I told my mom we had to quit buying grapes. She hardly ever bought them anyhow, she said, because they were expensive, but she promised not to buy them again until the strike was over.

When I was 17, I was a Stouffer Girl, a waitress at a classy restaurant in Oakland, the kind I had never been to before in my life. Our uniforms were red polyester and looked like airline hostess uniforms, and we had to stand in line for inspection every day. They made me wear a wig to cover up my hippie hair.

The trays were heavy and the work was hard. We worked split shifts, 10:30 in the morning until 2:30 in the afternoon and 5:30 until 8:30 in the evening. I had to take two buses to get to work so I left at 9 in the morning and didn't get home until 10 at night. The one saving grace was the free meal we got for every meal we worked, which included an appetizer and dessert. We ate in the kitchen, but they fed us the same delicious food the customers got.

ARE WE DONE
ALREADY?
I WANT MORE!

• • •

Choose one person and use the
People approach to write a deeper
story about them. Look for photos
that will represent different facets of
that person's life. Create a print book
for that person as a birthday gift, or a
slide show for their birthday party.

• • •

• • •

Use the **People** approach to write about your work life, tracing your career from the very beginning. List every job you've ever had, starting from the very first – your paper route, babysitting the neighbor's kids, earning a weekly allowance by cleaning your room.

• • •

• • •

Create a retirement gift for someone
by using the **People** approach to
write about their career. Ask lots of
questions and find out, step by step
from their first dollar earned, how
that person came to be where
they are today. Record what
they say, or take notes.

• • •

· · ·

Adapt the **Common Threads** approach to anything you like. Write about every family vacation you've ever had, from childhood to present day. Write about all the friends you've been close to over your life and the things you did together. Write about all the sports stadiums you've seen and the games you attended, the movie theaters you've gone to throughout your life and the movies you saw there that you'll never forget. Write about the museums you've visited and the amazing things in their collections. Write about all your favorite bookstores and the books you bought there, and what each book meant to you.

· · ·

• • •

Choose one of your family **Traditions** to examine in detail. Follow it through the years. Show how it was celebrated in the beginning and how it has changed over time.

• • •

• • •

Write a page about each of the
Family Values on your list. How
is that value demonstrated in your
family's day-to-day life?

• • •

• • •

Collect **How They Met** stories of
family members and their best
friends. Include the youngsters!

• • •

• • •

Collect stories from attendees at a
Big Event. Create a book about a
family wedding to give to the couple
for their anniversary. Collect stories
about a family reunion and share the
memories at the next reunion.

• • •

* * *

Collect stories of **Special Moments**
you've shared with your daughter, or
your uncle, or your close friend. When
your daughter graduates college,
or when your uncle or friend has a
milestone birthday, give them your
collection of those memories.

* * *

• • •

Ask family members about Mom's
special way of **Showing Love** to them.
Collect the stories to give to Mom
on Mother's Day.

• • •

• • •

Remember the box full of index
cards you inherited from Grandma,
full of **Family Recipes**? Make one
of those recipes, take a photo, and
create a page with a few sentences of
memories related to that food. Send
the page to your family members
along with the recipe.

• • •

• • •

Create a cookbook with your **Family Recipes**. You can even give it a theme, if you like, collecting traditional holiday recipes, or recipes from the last family reunion. Or ask family members to each choose a recipe for a Favorite Family Foods cookbook. Create a cookbook with meals and desserts you made for your kids while they were growing up, and give it to your son when he moves away from home.

• • •

● ● ●

Adapt the **Your Home As Family History** approach to tell the story of your life. Include every place you've lived for any length of time – even summer camp, your college dorm room, and the month you spent in Europe living out of a suitcase.

● ● ●

• • •

Use the questions in **Your Life Is Family History** to write your memoir.

• • •

There are a thousand ways to write your family story, so use this book as a jumping-off point.

Come up with your own lists of topics.

Create a new approach.

Call your grandma, or your oldest son, or your second cousin. Ask about their childhood, their teenage years. Ask about the biggest surprises and happiest moments in their adult lives.

Listen. Listen. Listen.

And then write it down.

THE MOST IMPORTANT THING TO REMEMBER

There's no wrong way to write
your family story.

It doesn't matter if it's perfect.

It only matters that you *do* it.

Appendix:
Creating a Book to Share

We've talked about PDFs before. They're a great way to share your story. They're compact and easy to manage. Your grandma can read a PDF on her computer, and your grandson can read a PDF on his phone.

You may want a physical book, though. One you can hold in your hand. So here are some simple ways to make that happen.

The easiest, and most obvious, is to print your pages and staple them together or put them in a binder.

A lovely old-fashioned method that is enjoying new popularity is the scrapbook. Print your pages, or even hand-write the stories with your photos.

Another option would be to send your pages to a local copy shop to have them printed on quality paper and bound.

For a more professional-looking book, search "photo books" online. You'll find companies that make personalized books. This is a great option if you want one book as a keepsake or for a gift.

If you want a box of books for a family reunion or other big event, search "small run book printing" online. You'll find companies that can supply your books at a reasonable cost, and many will bind a book that is not very long at all. DiggyPOD, for example, will print books as short as 16 pages.

If you'd like your book to be available to the general public, Amazon's Kindle Direct Publishing and IngramSpark are two popular print-on-demand services. The process can be complicated, but they give you step-by-step directions to offer your book for sale online.

Photo Credits

p 6   Courtesy of Aleksandar Andreev

p 7   Courtesy of Kulina Family ©2026

p 14   Courtesy of Paula Hahn ©2026

p 38   Courtesy of Kulina Family ©2026

p 39   Courtesy of Katelyn Warner

p 49   Courtesy of Elena Chertovskikh

p 50   Courtesy of Kulina Family ©2026

p 57   Courtesy of Mark Krchmar ©2026

p 58   Courtesy of Pixabay

p 63   Courtesy of Vincent Sebart

p 64   Courtesy of Ksenia Chernaya

p 71   Courtesy of Cade Martin

p 72   Courtesy of Les Anderson

p 78   Courtesy of Leeloo The First

p 79   Courtesy of Highwaystarz Photography

p 86   Courtesy of Jacob Lund

p 87   Courtesy of Frederick Wallace

p 94   Courtesy of Bess Hamiti

p 95   Courtesy of Mohamedamine Abbas

p 101   Courtesy of Cyrilla Bakey ©2026

p 102   Courtesy of Aunt Laya

p 110   Courtesy of Kulina Family ©2026

p 111   Courtesy of Kulina Family ©2026

p 118   Courtesy of Josef Schwarz, Creative Commons
        Attribution-Share Alike 3.0 Unported

p 119   Courtesy of Picryl

Heartfelt Thanks

To Lynda Barry and Nancy Slonim Aronie, who taught me to write with empathy, compassion and dignity.

To Chris Wells, who taught me to organize my thoughts and challenge my limits.

To Cyrilla Bakey, Sandie Earnest, Doug Edelson, Denise Guerringue and Nancy Kulina, who wrote their family stories to help me hone these approaches.

To all my students over the years. Thanks for the laughter and the tears we shared as we explored your memories.

To Scott Smith, the best editor ever.

And of course, as always, to my family.

About the Author

Anita Kulina grew up in Pittsburgh, Pennsylvania, where her father labored as a steelworker at the U.S. Steel Homestead Works while her mother chased around their six kids. Anita has always loved to write, even as a child kneeling at the coffee table in the family's living room. Her first publication was a letter to the editor in Adventure Comics #341.

Anita has been writing family histories, and coaching others in writing their family histories, for nearly thirty years. Her books include *Millhunks and Renegades: A Portrait of a Pittsburgh Neighborhood* and two cozy mysteries, *A Question of Devotion* and *Reason for Concern*.

www.ingramcontent.com/pod-product-compliance
Lightning Source LLC
Chambersburg PA
CBHW060236030426
42335CB00014B/1481